Information for Parents

In literacy lessons teachers will be seeking to encourage their pupils to:

- Read confidently and with understanding;
- Understand phonics and spelling patterns;
- Use neat handwriting with speed and accuracy;
- Expand their vocabulary;
- Appreciate a range of styles in fiction and poetry;
- Understand how stories are structured by the writers' use of settings, characters and plots;
- Read and use non-fiction materials;
- Develop their own writing using techniques of planning, drafting and editing;
- Enjoy reading books;
- Use imagination and inventiveness in their own writing.

Throughout the primary years the children will address their literacy work in two broad areas:

(i) Speaking and listening, through discussion, interaction and drama;

(ii) Reading and writing for a range of purposes on paper and on computer screen.

You can provide support to your children in the first of these areas by giving them lots of opportunities to speak to other people and to listen carefully in a range of situations.

Using the books in this **Literacy Now** series will give your children a wealth of extra support in the second area: reading and writing.

Through the series we provide practice materials for reading words and spelling them, understanding and responding to texts, developing well-structured sentences and using a range of punctuation correctly and effectively.

The books are matched appropriately to ages and are designed to be used by parents working with their children to provide extra practice, whether out of a need to improve particular aspects of English or simply for the fun of working on the subject at home.

Litera for ages 7-10

D0244276

Excellent practice for literacy

You may prefer to use this book as a textbook, rather than as a book to write in. If so, you will need to use an exercise book for your answers.

Try to work out the type of answer that is required for each question. Some questions just need single words for their answers; others need whole sentences. We sometimes provide two or more lines to write answers on, to give you clues as to how much you ought to write.

If you need help from an adult it is all right to ask for it. Sometimes you can learn a lot more just by having a small amount of help. It is always a good idea to have your work checked by an adult when you have finished it. If you have made mistakes you can learn from them.

Andrew Brodie

Jaz

Jaz was a rather lovely, pale golden hamster. At least, most people thought he was lovely. Aunty Joan didn't like him, as all furry animals made her shudder and she simply referred to him as 'that thing'. Cousin Ross wasn't a hamster fan either, saying that anything that small couldn't possibly be considered a first class pet. Amy, however, thought that Jaz was, without doubt, the most beautiful hamster in existence.

To live in, Jaz had what could only be described as a hamster mansion. This was situated in the corner of the sitting room. It consisted of several brightly coloured, hamster-sized rooms connected by a selection of tubular walkways (or in some cases, when placed vertically, 'climbways').

Each week Amy, helped (or sometimes hindered) by her younger brother Nick, would clean out 'Hamsterville' (as the living accommodation was affectionately known). All the bedding material was carefully emptied, each room and tube was cleaned thoroughly, fresh bedding was put in and then they enjoyed putting it all back together again in a new configuration.

Amy would then have the pleasure of watching Jaz exploring the new layout by running through the many pieces of translucent plastic tubing and deciding which room to store his food in and where to sleep.

Whatever Aunty Joan and cousin Ross might think, Amy knew that Jaz was an ideal pet in every way.

Jaz

1 Name the two people who were not convinced that Jaz was lovely.

Aunty Joan   _Cousin Ross_

2 Would Aunty Joan have liked a guinea pig better?
Give a reason for your answer.

She simply referred to him as that thing.

3 What type of pet might cousin Ross have preferred and why?

He wanted a first class pet because he's saying that anything that small couldn't possibly be considered.

4 What was the hamster housing known as in Amy's house?

Know as a hamster mansion.

You may
need a dictionary
to help you now.

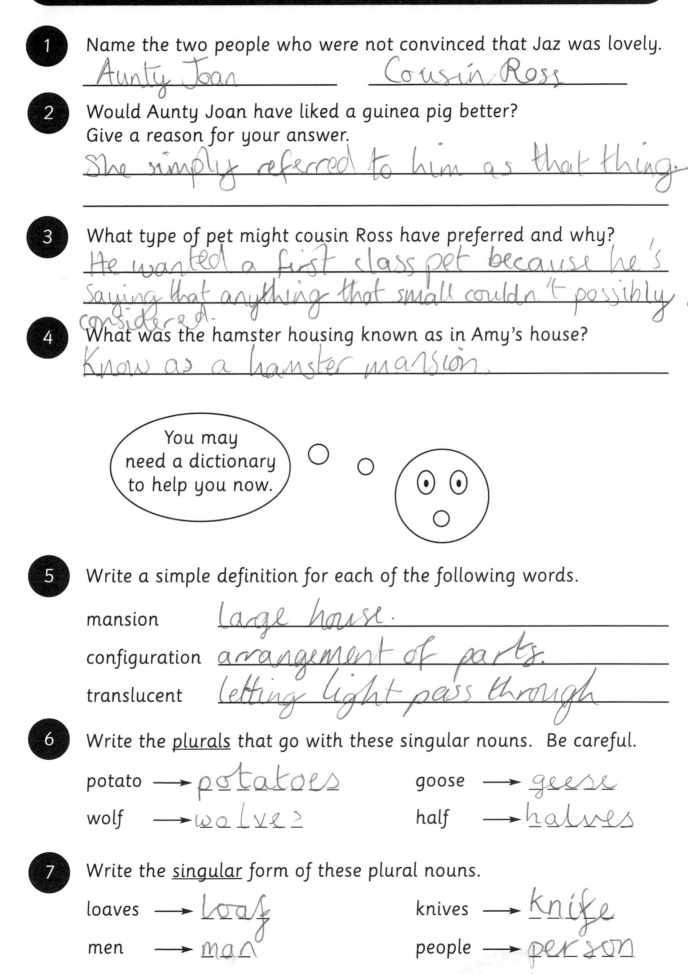

5 Write a simple definition for each of the following words.

mansion   _large house._

configuration   _arrangement of parts._

translucent   _letting light pass through_

6 Write the <u>plurals</u> that go with these singular nouns. Be careful.

potato ⟶ _potatoes_   goose ⟶ _geese_

wolf ⟶ _wolves_   half ⟶ _halves_

7 Write the <u>singular</u> form of these plural nouns.

loaves ⟶ _loaf_   knives ⟶ _knife_

men ⟶ _man_   people ⟶ _person_

Fire

For a few moments Maddie's mind went back to her childhood. She remembered with clarity the day she first noticed the flickering light of a candle. The way the flame would sway in a gentle draught, the blue colour in the centre of it and how dark smoke would curl when the candle was blown out. She also clearly recalled winter trips to her grandparents' house, where she loved to gaze at the open fire. Maddie had loved the way the fire crackled and flared, illuminating the whole room. She also remembered the sharp, stinging pain she had felt when a stray spark flew from the grate and struck her bare arm.

Maddie smiled as she thought about the time her parents were convinced she was terribly afraid of fireworks. Whilst her friends 'oohed' and 'aahed' at the sight of them, Maddie had just watched, solemn faced, in complete silence. It was quite a while before anyone realised that this was, in fact, because she was too engrossed to utter any sounds when she was trying to remember each coloured spark and starburst.

A frown briefly creased Maddie's brows as she remembered the time when people thought her fascination with fire could become a problem. But still, she thought, it had turned out very well in the end.

At that moment she was jolted back to reality as the engine stopped and, along with her colleagues, she quickly jumped down from the vehicle. As a fire fighter, she not only had the opportunity to see fires nearly every day but, more importantly, she could save both people and property by putting the fires out.

1 How are we told at the start of the text that Maddie is an adult?

_____

2 Why do you think that people thought Maddie's fascination with fire could become a problem?

_____

_____

3 Ring the word nearest in meaning to the following words taken from the text.

clarity

       fright   clearness   brightness   delight

brows

       forehead   hairline   eyebrows   face

colleagues

       friends   family   managers   workmates

4 Name the three types of fire that featured in Maddie's memories.

_____   _____   _____

Adverbs

Choose adverbs from the box to complete each of the following sentences in three different ways.
Use each adverb only once.

Adverbs are used to describe verbs. Most adverbs end in 'ly'.

ADVERBS
swiftly   softly   fearfully   briskly   crossly
longingly   excitedly   speedily   sadly

_____

She ran _____ along the street.

_____

_____

"Oh dear," he said _____ .

_____

_____

Will they be here soon? he wondered _____

_____

Idiomatic phrases

Read the sentences below. You will understand the meaning of each one, even though the well-known phrases that are underlined don't literally mean what they say.

Rewrite each sentence to say what is actually meant.
The first one has been done for you.

1 She was <u>tickled pink</u> when she received the prize.

She was delighted when she received the prize.

2 He visited the doctor as he was feeling rather <u>under the weather</u>.

_____

3 Without his glasses he was as <u>blind as a bat</u>.

_____

4 She felt like a <u>fish out of water</u> in the room full of boys.

_____

_____

_____

5 Her little brother was <u>driving her up the wall</u>.

_____

_____

_____

Proverbs

Proverbs are old sayings that contain a message or lesson.
For example:

<u>Proverb</u> ~ One man's meat is another man's poison.
<u>Meaning</u> ~ What suits one person may not suit another.

6

Proverbs

Choose the correct proverbs from the box to match the meanings given below.

> **PROVERBS**
> A bird in the hand is worth two in the bush.
> All that glitters is not gold.
> A stitch in time saves nine.
> Every cloud has a silver lining.
> Look before you leap.

Meaning – Give thought to your action before doing it.
Proverb – *Look before you leap*

Meaning – One thing now is better than the promise of more in the future.
Proverb – *A stich in time saves nine*

Meaning – A little work now can save a lot of work later.
Proverb – *A bird in the hand is worth two in the brush.*

Meaning – Things are not always as good as they look.
Proverb – *All that glitter is not gold*

Meaning – Difficult situations usually have a bright side too.
Proverb – *Every cloud has a silver lining*

Homophones

These are words that sound the same, but have different meanings and spellings,   e.g.   they're = they are   their = belonging to them
Choose the correct word to complete each sentence.

I saw a *plane* in the sky. | plane or plain |

The church bells *peal* on Sundays. | peel or peal |

The winner was given a gold *medal*. | medal or meddle |

The lion ran to catch its *prey*. | pray or prey |

Cod, *plaice* and herring are all types of fish. | place or plaice |

7

Cleaning the car

"Why don't you help clean the car?" suggested Mum.

"Good idea," squealed Maggie, quickly pulling on her Wellington boots and waterproof jacket.

"Watch out, trouble's on its way," called Mum to Dad from the kitchen window as little Maggie hurtled down the hall and out of the front door. Outside, Dad was washing the car down with a sponge soaked in warm soapy water from a large blue bucket.

"Where's my sponge?" asked Maggie.

"Here it is," replied Dad, patiently passing Maggie a sponge about half the size of the one he was using himself.

For the next few minutes Maggie busied herself cleaning one of the car wheels. Then, all of a sudden, a shriek of surprise was heard and Dad looked round to see what was happening.

Just as Dad realised what had occurred, Mum rushed out of the house. She had seen events unfolding from her vantage point by the kitchen window, and was now trying desperately to keep a straight face.

There, in the driveway, was a startled looking Maggie. She had slipped backwards and was now sitting wedged into the bucket of soapy water, quite unable to move.

1 In this text, the word 'said' has not been used to describe the talking. List below the five words used instead of 'said'.

_____   _____   _____

_____   _____

2 Explain why you think the author used these words instead of 'said'.

_____

_____

3 How can we tell that Maggie is quite young?

_____

_____

4 Explain how you know that Maggie's 'accident' caused amusement.

_____

_____

Cleaning the car

5   Maggie <u>hurtled</u> down the hall.
Ring the word nearest in meaning to hurtled.

       strolled   rushed   hassled   went

6   What is meant in the text by 'vantage point'?

_____

_____

Spelling tricky words

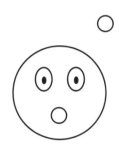

You may need a dictionary to help you with this.

The vowels have been missed out from the following words. See if you can fill them in correctly. There is a clue to help you work out what each word should be.

1. Paper, etc, is known as: s t _ t _ _ n _ r y

2. Necklaces, rings, etc: j _ w _ ll _ r y

3. Something or someone you know well is: f _ m _ l _ _ r

4. Left alone: _ b _ n d _ n _ d

5. Books are found here: l _ b r _ r y

Now put the missing vowels in the following sentences.

1. On W _ dn _ sd _ y m _ rn _ ng we have l _ t _ r _ cy, h _ st _ ry, m _ ths and r _ l _ g _ _ _ s ed _ c _ t _ _ n.

2. My best fr _ _ nd is always very good c _ mp _ ny.

9

Armies in the fire

This poem was written by Robert Louis Stevenson.
He lived in the 19th Century and wrote many poems for children.

The lamps now glitter down the street;
Faintly sound the falling feet;
And the blue even slowly falls
About the garden trees and walls.

Now in the falling of the gloom
The red fire paints the empty room:
And warmly on the roof it looks,
And flickers on the backs of books.

Armies march by tower and spire
Of cities blazing, in the fire;
Till as I gaze with staring eyes,
The armies fade, the lustre dies.

Then once again the glow returns;
Again the phantom city burns;
And down the red-hot valley, lo!
The phantom armies marching go!

Blinking embers, tell me true
Where are those armies marching to,
And what the burning city is
That crumbles in your furnaces?

1 In verse 1 line 3, the word 'even' is short for which word?

_____

2 Explain the two ways you know it is the evening after reading
only the first verse.

_____

_____

3 Which of the following best describes how the poem is written?

blank verse   free verse   rhyming couplets

Armies in the fire

4 Explain the line (in verse 2) that reads, 'The red fire paints the empty room'.

_____

_____

5 Explain how there are armies and cities in the fire.

_____

_____

6 In verse 4, why is the city in the fire called a 'phantom city'?

_____

_____

7 Which two-word phrase in the last verse tells us that the fire is dying? _____ _____

Write the words from the box in the correct lists.

You must put five words into each list.

television   rickety   sleepy
paper   ran   short   barn
colourful   sleeper   elderly
see   smiled   slept
laughing   chair

NOUNS	VERBS	ADJECTIVES
_____	_____	_____
_____	_____	_____
_____	_____	_____
_____	_____	_____
_____	_____	_____

11

Old Lion ~ a fable

A very elderly lion was feeling hungry. Unfortunately, Old Lion was too old and feeble to hunt successfully. He knew he faced a stark choice, eat or die. After many years of relying on his speed and strength he realised that, to survive, he must instead use his brain, which was luckily as nimble as ever.

After some hours spent deep in thought, he hatched a plan that, being extremely hungry, he put into action immediately. Old Lion feigned a severe illness, and soon his moaning could be heard for miles around. Hearing his pitiful cries the other animals were soon feeling very sorry for him.

"Perhaps we should visit Old Lion," they said.

On hearing this Old Lion, in a weak and trembling voice, called, "I can't cope with a crowd. Just call in one at a time if you would be so kind."

First went Zebra, a little later Baboon, next Gazelle and fourthly Snake slithered towards Old Lion. Fox watched all this thoughtfully, as it was his turn to visit next. Fox moved towards Old Lion's den, but stopped several metres from the entrance.

"Please come close, old friend," pleaded Old Lion, "I cannot see you properly out there."

"I think it would be most unwise of me to come any closer," replied Fox, "for I can see four sets of tracks leading into your cave but none coming out again. To be sure to live another day, I will stay well away from you – just as all the others should have done."

1. Write the two words in the first sentence that tell you of the lion's great age. _elederly._

2. Ring the words nearest in meaning to 'stark choice'.

a happy choice   a choice about food

a clear cut choice   (a choice about animals)

12

Old Lion ~ a fable

3 Ring the word nearest in meaning to 'feigned.'

(faked)   caught   felt   hurt

4 Why did Old Lion put his plan into action immediately?

Because instead of him catching he bring the one at the time.

5 Why did Old Lion want to see the animals one at a time?

Because he couldn't be bother to catch.

6 Ring the correct lesson that could be learned from this fable.

(Slow but steady wins the race.)

Don't pretend to be what you are not.

Think for yourself rather than just follow others.

Plurals

Follow this rule for words ending in 'y'.

A 'y' after a vowel = add <u>s</u> e.g. **day** becomes **days**

A 'y' after a consonant = take off the 'y' and add <u>ies</u> e.g. **baby** → **babies**

Write the plural of each of the following words.

fly _flies_   tray _trays_

jelly _jellis_   city _cities_

holiday _holidays_   spray _sprays_

cry _cries_   boy _boys_

puppy _puppies_   party _parties_

13

Fascinating facts

On this page you will find a display of fascinating facts about famous people in history. Read them carefully and then answer the questions.

Francis Drake circumnavigated the world during the reign of Elizabeth I.

Elizabeth I reigned from 1558 to 1603.

'The Water Babies' was a novel written by the Victorian author Charles Kingsley.

A Russian cosmonaut called Yuri Gagarin made the first manned space flight.

Queen Victoria reigned from 1837 to 1901.

Christopher Columbus, the famous explorer, sailed to America in 1492.

ALEXANDER GRAHAM BELL INVENTED THE TELEPHONE DURING THE REIGN OF QUEEN VICTORIA.

King Henry VIII married six times.

Charles Dickens, a famous Victorian author, wrote many classic books including Nicholas Nickleby and A Christmas Carol.

Pythagoras was a Greek philosopher and mathematician.

1　Name the famous Greek mathematician.　_Pythagorus_

2　Name the three monarchs mentioned in the historical facts.

King Henry VIII　　_Elizabeth I_　　_Queen Victoria_

Fascinating facts

3 Who was the first person in space? _Yuri Gagarin_

4 Who sailed around the world? _Christopher Columbus_

5 Name three novels written during the reign of Queen Victoria.
Christmas Carols   _Nicholas Nickeby_
The Water Babies

6 Which famous explorer travelled to America and when did he do this? _Christopher Columbus sailed in 1492_

7 How many facts can be found on the previous page? _10_

8 Which monarch reigned for over sixty years? _Victoria_

9 Name a Victorian inventor and his invention.
Alexander Graham Bell   _telephone_

Sort the words from the box into nouns, verbs and adjectives.

reading   wide   builder   hairy   be
street   banana   London   beautiful
sitting   run   snoring   wishing   crunchy
wildhouse   sleeve   expensive

Nouns	Verbs	Adjectives
builder	reading	wide
street	be	hairy
banana	sitting	beautiful
London	run	crunchy
wildhouse	snoring	expensive
sleeve	wishing	wishing

15

Making a rubbed wax picture

You will need:
2 pieces of paper (1 sugar/1 fine) identical in size.
1 wax crayon
sugar paper for cutting into smaller pieces
1 pair scissors
glue for sticking paper

(1) Use 1 piece of plain sugar paper for the background.

(2) Cut individual items from sugar paper, such as trees, clouds, etc.

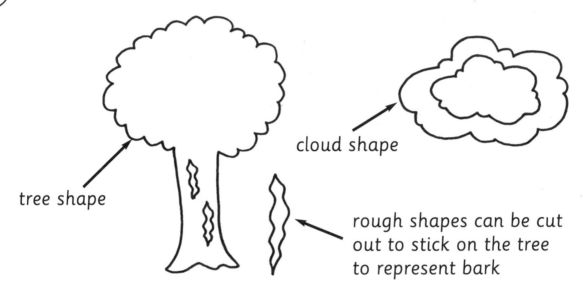

tree shape

cloud shape

rough shapes can be cut
out to stick on the tree
to represent bark

(3) Use extra layers of sugar paper to create areas that will be darker
when rubbing is completed. The more layers you add, the darker
the area will be.

(4) Stick the individual items onto the background paper.

(5) Place the fine paper over the picture.

(6) Using the side of a wax crayon, carefully rub the whole of the
paper exerting an even pressure.

Now answer these questions.

1 Why have the instructions been numbered?

_____

_____

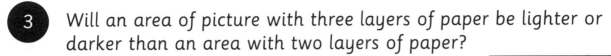

Making a rubbed wax picture

2 Does it matter what colour sugar paper you use? Explain your answer.

_____

_____

3 Will an area of picture with three layers of paper be lighter or darker than an area with two layers of paper? _____

4 In your own words explain what is meant by 'rub the whole of the paper exerting an even pressure'.

_____

_____

Prefixes

Read the prefixes and their meanings.

bi = two   tri = three   quad = four

Now put in the correct prefix to label each picture.

_____dent

_____ cycle

_____ ruplets

_____kini

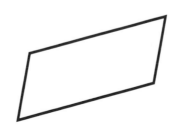

_quad_rilateral

_quad_cycle

17

Seven young owls

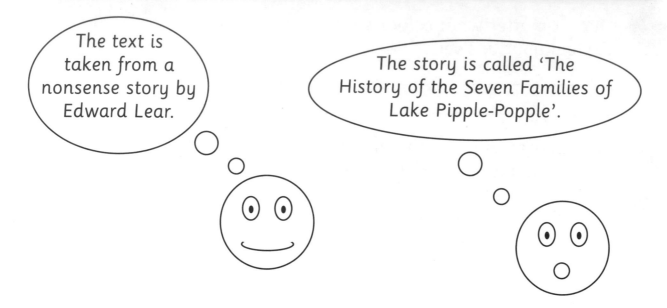

The text is taken from a nonsense story by Edward Lear.

The story is called 'The History of the Seven Families of Lake Pipple-Popple'.

Chapter VIII
The History of the Seven Young Owls

When the seven young owls set out, they sat every now and then on the branches of old trees, and never went far at one time.

And one night, when it was quite dark, they thought they heard a mouse, but as the gas lamps were not lighted, they could not see him. So they called out, 'Is that a mouse?'

On which a mouse answered, 'Squeaky-peeky-weeky, yes it is.'

And immediately all the young owls threw themselves off the tree, meaning to alight on the ground; but they did not perceive that there was a large well below them, into which they fell superficially, and were every one of them drowned in less than half a minute.

So that was the end of the Seven Young Owls.

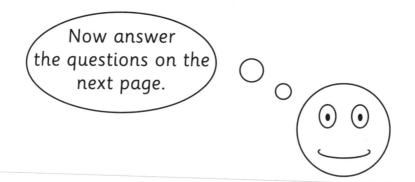

Now answer the questions on the next page.

Seven young owls

1 How do we know the owls are not adults?

_____

2 Which chapter of the story is the text from? (Ring the correct answer)

    chapter four   chapter six   chapter eight

3 Edward Lear lived from 1812 to 1888. What is the clue in the text that tells us this is not a modern story?

_____

4 Ring the word closest in meaning to 'alight'.

    land   skid   perch   bounce

5 Ring the word closest in meaning to 'perceive'.

    prefer   notice   land   allow

6 What happened to all seven owls in the end?

_____

i before e

Many words have 'ie' in them.

1. Look at each of these words.
2. Cover it.
3. Write it.
4. Check to see if you spelled it correctly.

shield	relief	fierce
_____	_____	_____
yield	niece	pie
_____	_____	_____
tie	thief	field
_____	_____	_____

Seven young fishes

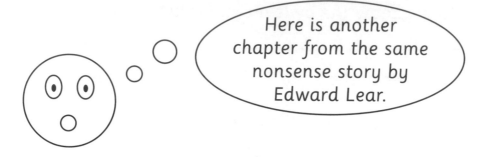

Here is another chapter from the same nonsense story by Edward Lear.

Chapter XI
The History of the Seven Young Fishes

The seven young fishes swam across the Lake Pipple-Popple and into the river and into the ocean where, most unhappily for them they saw, on the fifteenth day of their travels, a bright-blue Boss-Woss, and instantly swam after him. But the Blue Boss-Woss plunged into a
        perpendicular,
           spicular,
              orbicular,
                 quadrangular,
                     circular depth of soft mud,
where in fact his house was.

And the seven young fishes, swimming with great and uncomfortable velocity, plunged also into the mud, quite against their will, and, not being accustomed to it, were all suffocated in a very short period.

And that was the end of the Seven Young Fishes.

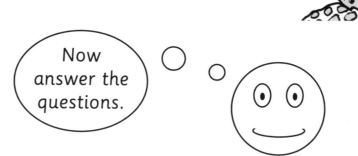

Now answer the questions.

1   What did the seven fishes see on the fifteenth day of their travels?

_____

2   What words are used in the text to describe the mud?

_____

3 What is meant by the phrase 'great and uncomfortable velocity'?

_____

4 How did the fish die?

_____

The suffix 'ful' means full.

When added to a word ending in a consonant followed by y, the y is changed to an i.

Complete the pairs below. The first two pairs have been done for you.

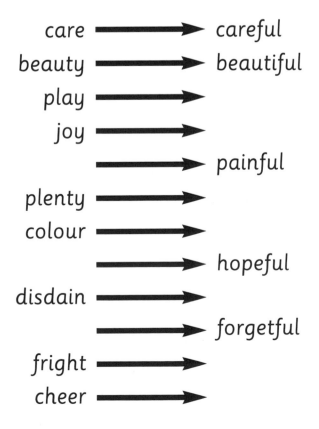

care ⟶ careful

beauty ⟶ beautiful

play ⟶

joy ⟶

⟶ painful

plenty ⟶

colour ⟶

⟶ hopeful

disdain ⟶

⟶ forgetful

fright ⟶

cheer ⟶

Black Beauty

'Black Beauty' is a novel by Anna Sewell.
This story was written as if by the horse himself.

Chapter One
<u>My Early Home</u>

The first place that I can well remember was a large pleasant meadow with a pond of clear water in it. Some trees overshadowed the pond, and rushes and water-lilies grew at the deep end. Over the hedge on one side we looked into a ploughed field; and on the other, we looked over a gate at our master's house which stood by the roadside. At the top of the meadow was a plantation of fir trees; and at the bottom, a running brook overhung by a steep bank.

Whilst I was young I lived upon my mother's milk, as I could not eat grass. In the daytime I ran by her side, and at night I lay down close by her. When it was hot, we used to stand by the pond in the shade of the trees; and when it was cold, we had a nice warm shed near the plantation.

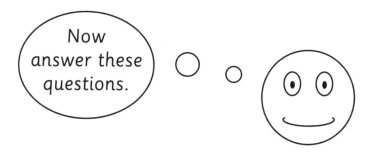

Now answer these questions.

1   Name two features that could be found in the meadow.

Pond

water-lilly

2   What could be found at the top of the meadow?

The trees.

3   What could be found at the bottom of the meadow?

road

Black Beauty

4 At one side of the meadow (over the hedge) was a ploughed field. What could be seen on the other side (over the gate)?

The grass.

5 Where did the horses shelter in cold weather?

In the plantation.

6 How did the horses keep cool in hot weather?

Go and stand by in the pond.

Read the text again and use it to help you draw an illustration below.

Ben's racquet (part 1)

Ben played tennis. While many of his friends preferred football, rugby or swimming, Ben took great delight in heading for the tennis courts.

He belonged to a local club and he had heard one of the coaches tell his parents that he 'showed great promise'. Ben wasn't sure exactly what that meant but he knew it was good. He dreamed of one day lifting the men's singles' trophy at Wimbledon.

Next week was Ben's birthday. Each time his parents asked what he would like he shrugged and said he wasn't sure. The truth was that he had seen a wonderful new tennis racquet in the sports shop window, but he knew it was far too expensive to ask Mum and Dad to buy. Each time he passed the shop he looked at the racquet, but he was careful not to say anything.

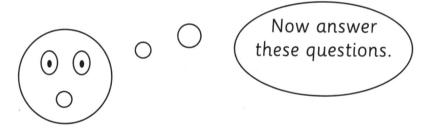

Now answer these questions.

1 Name Ben's favourite sport.

Tennis

2 What did Ben's coach mean by 'showed great promise'?

It means he did really good

3 What does a tennis coach do?

Play proper tennis.

Ben's racquet (part 1)

4 Why didn't Ben want to ask his parents to buy the new racquet for his birthday?

Because he doesn't say anything.

5 Do you think that Ben should have told his parents the truth?

Yes, but he doesn't want to give it away.

Singular and plural

Look at the words in the box. They are all plurals.

> 1) babies 7) matches 8) potatoes
> 6) loaves 4) knives 2) calves 11) watches
> 9) scarves 10) tomatoes 12) wives
> 3) churches 5) ladies

In the spaces below, write the <u>singular</u> of each word. Arrange your list in <u>alphabetical</u> order. The first one has been done for you.

1 baby
2 _calf_
3 _church_
4 _knife_
5 _lady_
6 _loaves_

7 _matches_
8 _potatoes_
9 _scarves_
10 _tomatoes_
11 _watches_
12 _wives_

Ben's racquet (part 2)

It was Ben's birthday. He hoped that his parents and grandparents might give him some money. Then, if he continued to save his pocket money, in a few weeks he might have enough for the gleaming new racquet he had seen.

His parents had a small wrapped parcel for him. It was a computer game, a rather smaller gift than usual but Ben knew that there was little spare money in the household. He managed to look very pleased with it.

After school Ben, Mum and Dad walked through the town to tea with his grandparents. On his way past the sports shop, Ben glanced in the window. The racquet had gone. Despite his bitter disappointment, Ben reasoned that he had, as yet, no money towards it. Owning the racquet was nothing more than a pipedream.

He had a pleasant tea with his grandparents. They had bought him some tennis balls and made his favourite meal, after which they had a birthday cake with ten candles.

At eight o'clock it was time to go home. Ben was sent to fetch coats from the cupboard. He opened the door, where he stood mouth gaping in amazement. There stood the new racquet with a tag on it. The tag said, 'A surprise from Mum, Dad, Nanny and Grandad – Happy Birthday Ben'.

At last Ben turned to see his parents and grandparents watching him and smiling.

"How did you know?" he asked.

"We saw the way you looked each time you passed the shop window," said Dad, "and your coach said it would be ideal for you."

It was definitely, thought Ben as he fell asleep that night, the most marvellous birthday surprise.

Ben's racquet (part 2)

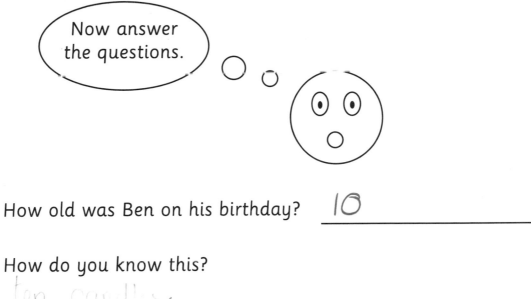

Now answer the questions.

1 How old was Ben on his birthday? _10_

2 How do you know this?

ten candles.

3 Explain the meaning of the word 'pipedream'.

Dream that.

4 How had Ben hoped to be able to afford the racquet?

save

5 Where had the racquet been 'hidden' for Ben to find later?

cupboard.

6 Why do you think his grandparents and parents were watching him when he opened the cupboard?

Because it was a surprise.

Holidays

Below are some competition entries. The competition, run by an international airline, was to win a holiday for two people. To enter the competition the entrant had to say, in a maximum of twenty words, where they would like to go and why.

Here are the four entries the judges liked most.

1.
> Icebergs,
> Cold water,
> Cruising here,
> With son and daughter.
> Whale watching
> From a boat,
> Alaska is where
> We'd be afloat.

2.
> Scuba diving,
> Hot springs,
> Mountains, valleys,
> Lord of the Rings.
> Golden beaches,
> Thermal steam,
> Going to New Zealand
> Would fulfil my dream.

3.
> Relaxation in the sun,
> Sports and swimming would be fun.
> Sandy beaches, swaying palms,
> West Indies, full of tropical charms.

4.
> Visit the Palace,
> Stroll in the parks.
> Busy daytime,
> Busy after dark.
> Many museums,
> Sights to see.
> In London town
> I'd like to be.

Holidays

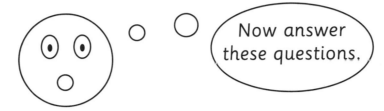

Now answer
these questions.

1 What do the four entries all have in common?

_____

_____

2 When the judges met to pick a winner, two of the entries were
immediately disqualified. Which ones and why?

_____

_____

3 After a great deal of thought, the judges gave the prize to entry
number 3. Why do you think they decided against the other
possible winner?

_____

_____

4 Where was the chosen destination of the people who wanted to
see thermal springs? _____

5 Which destination boasts a palace and many museums?

_____

6 Where might a whale watching cruise take place? _____

Write a short rhyming poem
(20 words or less) about
somewhere you would like to
visit. Sorry – we don't have
any prizes!

_____

_____

_____

_____

_____

_____

_____

_____

Holiday diary

Here is a small part of the holiday diary written by Shayla Rowe, who won the competition and enjoyed a wonderful vacation in the West Indies. She was accompanied by her friend Kim. They went in early June.

Tuesday 3rd

We landed in Antigua this afternoon and were taken by taxi to our hotel. Our room is lovely and the view out to sea quite spectacular. I've never seen such beautiful shades of blue in the water before. Had a lovely meal this evening in the open air restaurant – luckily there's no sign of rain!

Must take a picture of our room from the pool area tomorrow so we can show all our friends where we stayed.

Wednesday 4th

Took loads of photos this morning. Made a point of getting a picture of the room from the pool area. Kim stood on the balcony so it was obvious which room was ours.

Had a great day being thoroughly lazy.
Did the following: took photos, swam in sea, swam in pool, lazed under a sunshade, read a book, ate and drank!

This is the life!

Now answer the questions.

Holiday diary

1 Who wrote the holiday diary? _____

2 On what island were they staying? _____

3 What date did they arrive there? _____

4 What adjective describes the view out to sea? _____

5 What adjective describes the hotel room? _____

6 Why was it lucky that there was no rain on Tuesday evening?

_____

_____

_____

7 What does Shayla do to show all her friends where she stayed?

_____

_____

_____

8 What would make it clear on the photos which was their room?

_____

_____

_____

9 Why did Shayla put a colon after the words 'Did the following'?

_____

_____

_____

10 Explain the phrase 'This is the life'.

_____

_____

_____

My diary

Do you keep a diary?

It's a great way of keeping a record of your thoughts, feelings and events in your life.

Try keeping a diary for a week. Write down something for every day. Every day should have something special about it.

SUNDAY   Chilling out in the mornings and Karaté in the evening.

MONDAY   Urg!! Monday, going to school, Violin lessons. thats good

TUESDAY   Yum! Tuesday, FT, Food Technology, Cooking Delicious, and swimming. Splash!

WEDNESDAY   Going in 5, 4, 3, 2, 1, just joking, Science thats why.

THURSDAY   What do you think?, Just practising for ART. And then DRAMA. lights, Camera, Action.

FRIDAY   Yay! Schools nearly over but in the afternoon we get to watch, ATLANTIS!

SATURDAY   Yawn! Waking in the morning. GREAT! isn't it.